SPECIAL EDITION

THE

MODERN

HEART

ASHLEY POETRY

INTRODUCTION

I hope this book finds you well, happy and peaceful. maybe blissful and full of joy. perhaps this book has found you full of sorrow and pain, unknown grief, and cold desires unfulfilled. know this. the other side of either is just the other side. so you must know, right here in this ever-transforming moment, there is love. true love doesn't have a side. the most gentle beauty and the hardest form of ugly, look close enough and you will find love in every cell of it. you may want to argue with me and that's okay because love doesn't mind how you show up. a belly full of rage, decades of war, and love doesn't bat an eye. every heartbreak and soft tear, love, is right there. love is right here. love doesn't need you to believe me or believe in it. put your hands on your ribcage, feel the gift of life moving in and out of your body. feel your heart rhythmically beating and know, right here, now, is
l   o   v   e

THE MODERN HEART

I.

THE MODERN HEART

unabridged

even in suffering
let beauty in

one day this moment
will be the nostalgia

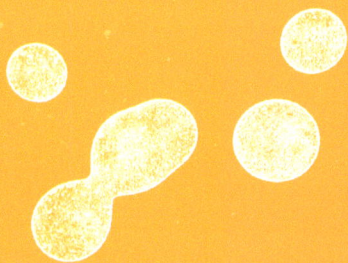

love is in the mirror
looking back at you

wrap your arms around loneliness
until you are hugging yourself

forgive every part
until you remember you are whole

look through my eyes
see how beautiful you are

do things when you are afraid
remember you are brave

when someone leaves
let them go
the only one who belongs to you is you
the rest is something else

if you want to leave
leave
make the decision and the world shifts
take all the time you need
you know when your moment is here
walk away and say thank you
to yourself
to your heart that is still beating
to your life that is unfolding

maybe you can't forget how
to love someone else
but you can remember how
to love yourself

life can be hard
it's harder if you don't feel
it makes you harder
still and stiff
inflexible things fall right
over in the wind

be flexible
swaying in the storms
grows deep roots

even trees that get blown
over start growing toward the sky
even trees that get struck
by lightning are beautiful

when the wave knows
she is the ocean
there is no discord
only storms and rainbows
and depth

the doctor told me
the only way to get rid of the pain
was to let our story go

but i can't let you go so easily
i won't
so i write you letters
and i yell at you in the dark
and there you are whispering
and shining a light

and suddenly we are under
the sheet fort we made
and suddenly we are laughing
on your roof
we watch the stars at night
together planning
how we want to see them
from the sand
and snow around a fire

and we agreed we want to see
them from above
calling ourselves our old names
the ones we knew from before
i blink my eyes open again
under a ceiling that seems
to be crumbling

(continued)

maybe i like pain
maybe i like it as much as you
but i want to be unfrozen
and move again
i want to allow myself
to be seen again
vulnerable without the armor
of stories and feelings

i want to be seen beyond you
so i write a book
i'll let you out of my body
and onto the pages
the ink pours from my rib cage
nectar from my heart

and now i hold you
in front of my chest
or flip through your pages
and see our names
strung together like a paper garland
paper cut into hearts
and bound together
i can set you down

yet you will live
i promised you how i love

i won't let love die
true love never dies

you could never understand
why i collected fossils and feathers
you wanted to believe
but would never open your eyes

shut so tight
i would navigate
from the wrong side of the car
the wrong side of the street

stuffing your fingers
inside my mouth
eyes growing wide
round and wider still

lips parting open
everything is moist
the air and lips and
drops from your forehead

we stained the rocks with love
planes flying
watching over our heads
waves crashing

(continued)

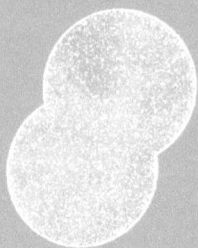

and you didn't bother
how much skin was lost
only that you controlled the end
and i pretended not to be hurt
flying toys through the air

checking steam train schedules
making sure we didn't pay extra
for jam and clotted cream
and i'm just trying to check-in

early to the next hotel
and i'm just trying to check in
how does my body feel
where in my body do i feel

does my body
remember to be feeling
how do i know
what i am feeling
feeling feelings and memories
memories and stored stories

forgive yourself a thousand times
this is called self love

put some makeup on or don't wear any
wear pretty underwear or none
take yourself to eat at a nice place
to savor the quiet or noise
and enjoy your legs touching each other

go dance just dance go home alone
or with someone if it feels good
no matter what look in the mirror
say i love you and thank you
a few times in the morning

there are many forms of self care

i am still learning
(how to play)
(that it will all be okay)
(how to walk as forgiveness)
(fill in the blank)

do you mind if i spend a lifetime
searching for my heart?

i am not here waiting
for something more
i am searching for the
littlest smallest hidden
pockets of love
that live in this life
that makes home in
what we call loneliness
that makes love in
what we call despair
and hope
i have met you in my dreams
i fall asleep and feel you with me
i drive my car and you
watch me dance and sing
i want to stop this maddening pace
and you take me to the mirror
to see you in my face

your name
was on everyone's lips and hearts
and now only in whispers
what happens when you die?
do you fade into the air?

i won't let you go so easily
so quickly
every beat of my heart
your name gets louder
in my ears
i look from your eyes now

when i hate everything
i think of how you would love this
then i feel you suddenly in the room
beyond the room

(continued)

i feel you well up in my eyes
thankful to feel bones again
to watch children grow again
like this
full of dull pain
loving so much it hurts all over
because this time is already away
this time is already different

you are gone
so you occupy the space
in between my eyebrows
you come and sit
on the top of my head
pretending to control me
pretending we are different

i'll make all these promises
i will be old and grey for you
wrinkled and brittle
one day for you
i'll live to be one hundred
and eight for you
for you
i promise to dance and sing
put my feet in wet grass
swim in our special place
make the world our special place
i'll breathe for you
i'll inhale and exhale everything
and write you letters and words
send you notes like you
were reading them
because you read them
please let me know you read them

(continued)

i promise
one day i'll stop
crying for you
and start only
smiling for you
i'll eat fruits in
season for you
for you
i'll close my eyes and taste
juice on my lips
you on my lips
fruit on my lips
maybe i'll eat the skins too
like i was brand new
i promise
i'll feel this world
like i was brand new
every note of this song
i promise
is for you

the things i am trying to say to you
can never be explained
but i keep searching
for the combination of letters
numbers perhaps
the metaphors of the golden bridge
from my heart to yours

the moon and i have inside jokes now
silence is our secret language
about the ways we both love
and the ways we never stop changing
how we both own the sea
how we both like the unfolding

then i'll hear music that talks
to me like you used to
a particular breeze and i smell you
i just want to read you the poetry
and for you to be able to listen
and here alive again
like in this way alive
touching me and laughing
at my jokes
telling me your plans
to rise early no matter how late
you find slumber
in the cold sheets
flip the pillow in your sleep
flip me over when you awake
we drop into a dream
state to meditate
on our lines and we play pretend
imagine where we start and end
what happened for
anything to begin

(continued)

do we need to wash
any clothes or uniforms
dry them on the line
in the front yard
colored clothespins
in soft paper bags
pin them up
sun time
for some time
then take them down
before it's too dark
i want to be naked
and unashamed
unhinged but fully aware
fully knowing with no memories
sewing together soft clothes
and white rags
golden threads and learning
sacred stitches
making sails for the boats
we stopped using oars
we stopped using ors
maybes and conclusions
just ands and inclusions
we want to have all experiences
all the opportunities to expand
and make ways for the story
that never ends

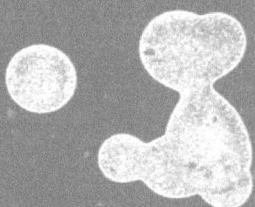

trust the sadness
it is the cleansing
trust the heartbreak
it is the opening
trust the clearing
it is the wildfires
trust the dreams
it is the messengers
trust the growing
it is the blooming
you are becoming
love

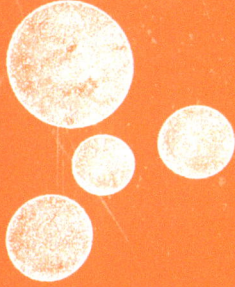

i won't be sad to have only a season with you
watching trees shed their leaves
the branches adorned with frozen rain
just touching a new bloom
bursting with life
rolling in the fields of wildflowers
only once
can change your heart

dear pain
you are temporary
you make me stronger
you allow me to grow
you show me where i am hurting
you bring me closer to myself
you are my secret keeper
you are my fable teller
thank you for being my teacher
i still always love you

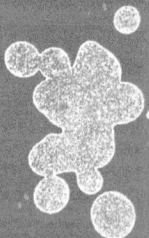

i can't survive in shortness
of breath
of feelings
of depth
of love stories

i like them to be full of dramatics
cliff hangers
epics
does one ever stop exhaling?
will i ever take another breath?

can i
can you
please stop walking away
deaths and rebirths
watching with new eyes

please wash my eyes
won't you?
transformations
everything transforming
happily ever afters too

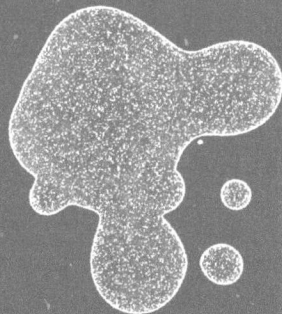

i can't stop writing you letters
i can't stop singing our songs
i don't care about formalities and rsvps
i don't care if i cry about everything
there is a dream after this one
there is a life after this one
maybe it's more real than your nightmares
maybe it's more than you could imagine
perhaps i decided to play in the wet grass
perhaps i decided to do laundry at the shore
sometimes i wonder if my cat feels my heart
sometimes i wonder if you read my mind
then i realize the falling stars are not stars
then i realize the river is my home
my grandfather's garden is overgrown now
my grandmother's heart is with me now
my children carry them in their bones now
my life is because of theirs now
my blood is thick like god's now

love isn't a question

if there is a question
love is the answer

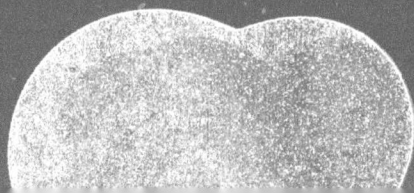

why does my shirt still smell like you
i washed it again
press the fabric to my face
like sandpaper on my lips
exfoliation and blood

why do my fingers still long for your spine
i stay awake all night again
press the dark sky into the spaces between
you and i
long distance calls

why are my feet still stained with your pollen
i walked the turtle back to the water again
press the mud into hand and shell
remembering being lost
sounds and sensations

why are words still being created
i wonder if we see the same color blue
press purple and yellow together
matching the sky at sunset
a golden hue

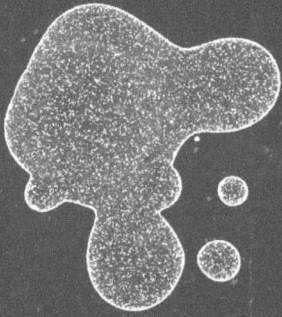

missing you
missing what we share
our love lives in the air

and i can't help
but let myself wander
into the thoughts of how
we will meet again
will the grass be wet with dew
or burned from the sun?
at the river or where it is dry?
the desert and we find the oasis
how many wrinkles and lovers
will we have acquired?
will our eyes still be a mirror?
will our hearts be open still?

no matter
how long
i stay in bed
the wildflowers
bloom still

we are timeless
boulders to pebbles
pebbles to smaller pebbles
tumbling still
dreaming of becoming sand
the sounds under the water
better than the symphony
we sat towards the back
here i am naked
underdressed
and there is no intermission

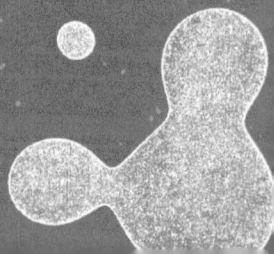

i keep going back
to the place we met
searching for you
swaying hips
dancing feet
kissing lips
holding hands

but nobody has your eyes
nobody has your eyes

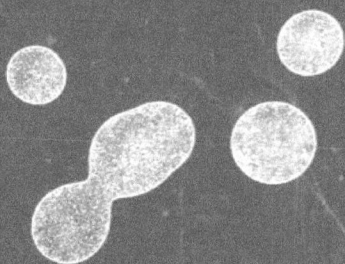

no gardens bloom
without your love
my ears become deaf
without your song
grey skies and seasons
stop turning

some days i just sit
and read all my poetry
sometimes i swear
it's your only gift to me

all i start to know is how i feel alone
my neighbor keeps mowing the flowers
before they bloom

one seeds finds a crack
in the driveway for next spring
they only bloom for a month
and smell like grape medicine
i want to taste them
my fingers won't even
pick up the smell
when i rub them so
so i see a spider
almost invisible
but i have the right light
and she climbs up her silk
into her flower home
only for a month
only for a season

one time i was walking
in the desert
i drank all the water
lost my way to the springs
the birds starting singing
about death
so i lay down in the sand
crying
so i could drink tears
do you understand
what heaven tastes like?
do you understand
what it takes to just be?

i will tell you all the secrets
but maybe
the greatest one is this
we each must
find our own way
don't believe anything i say
you won't really anyway
think and seek for yourself
there is one destination
endless trails to get there
the path isn't
marked anywhere
only inside your heartplace

i pray to become patience
she is the knowing
she is the practice
she is the bliss

she teaches us
the brightest sun
the longest day
the biggest shadows
all they want to do is play

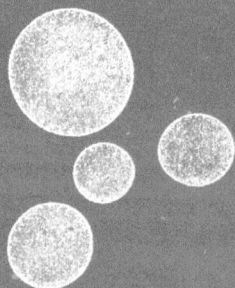

my love for you doesn't stop
because you left my side
my love doesn't know
your lips prefer another's
my love doesn't listen
when told to be contained
my love won't stop singing
about the depth of her ocean
my love doesn't ask questions
this love is only supreme

i keep looking
in the crowd for you
i keep surrendering
to my knees for you
crawling around
on the concert floor
looking for my glasses
they are tinted with roses
and smell like cotton candy
you smell like the present moment
i like when we smell like each other
and love making
and swapped fluids and screams
i can't find where my heart
pulls apart anymore
from yours
from the lies i tell myself
this searching is always
the lies i tell the air
we aren't scared of anything
any nightmare is really a dream

there is no other than now
i am only living now
i am only dying now
there is fire and smoke
and ember and ashes
there is lightning now
cicadas shaking in their shells
unearthing from illusion
just to fly for a day
then to die
but that's not the word they use
freedom is the closest i can find
nature does not die
there is no other than transforming
the moon is only lit by the sun
shadowed by life
we are the formless one

don't search for love
it's already found you

trying is the only resistance
intentional effort
heart centered surrender
full of purpose
soft like love
listen like this
embody the messenger
merge
into your body

breathe the parts of you
someone said where not enough
light up your gifted existence
enlightenment is compassion
spirituality is sexuality
your heart is your identity

if you hide your inner being
how will you ever be free?

your struggles don't define you
your strength does
when are you going to say
"i've had enough pretending
i am not enough?"

and what if this was it?
what if this is everything?
this moment
the endless exploration
this electrical fire
the fires
the sins
the sensations
the pains so great
the same as the darkness
the torture we seek
somehow it will save us
from ourselves
from this moment
we keep beating
until there is nothing left but the pulp
the pulse
the beating
of our hearts

we plant a garden
then maybe call it a farm
a few fruit pits become an orchard
we laugh
about the life we would plant
and now we stand in the dark soil
under our feet roots growing profound
watered by our tears from laughing
and memories examined again
both cleanse both grow seeds the same
and the rain watches us
and washes us too
our hands like vines
climbing into each other
into every open space
to fill it with passion
and flowers
the ones that turn into fruit
to be eaten
by the birds black and blue
red ones and their families
some carry the seeds so far
and some buried again close to home
i want to be buried close to here
but i wouldn't be sad if
i was carried away
my soul scattered somewhere new

who am i without these
scars and ashes?
tell me another definition of holy
these are sacred stories

i write you notes
fold them so particularly
like i am going to pass them
to you in the halls
i smile even though
i thought about dying
this morning and too much maybe
i hug others knowing they are you
i look at myself in the mirror
because i know you like to
see me that way
looking from my eyes
howling from my throat
all the secrets you already know

legs intertwined
why won't my
lips stop quivering?
why does my
heart keep beating?
closing eyes
softening to the edges
endings
new beginnings
cliches
happy endings

what is that rare flower sensation?

she is the one seeking the sun
she is the one seeking the moon

rainstorms find her
just the idea of her petals
one raindrop sliding down her curves
clouds travel over oceans
hoping to gather what she needs

she is the one who made
this empty lot a meadow
she is the one who makes
friends with the deer
and the skunks
beauty is in the darkest places
rain and dirt make mud
it's a spa day if you rub it on your faces

my first love
is it selfish to say
my own body
the way we play
she isn't explanation or words
do not trap her like a caged bird
the only label is a work of poetry
vibrating the formless finitely
skins of scars from
scrapes and scratches
rolling down hills of sunlit grasses
or morning dew covering
every part of me
learning to become
mostly to just be
cellular structures cannot define
everything i left behind
unlocking the codes
dancing the bones
shifting structures calling it alchemy
just humming to know the feeling
this body my offering
to experience love unapologetically

you are enough
you are enough
you offer your heart
so that is always enough

have you ever seen a light
that did not cast a shadow?

you are a vessel
not a container
do not close
and hold your experiences
stay open
allow life to flow through you
this is how love likes to find you
in fluidity

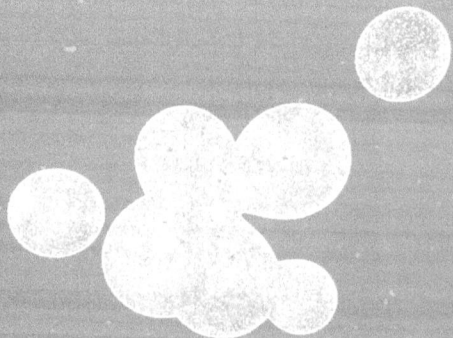

you are not loved
that's past tense
you are now
you are present
a gift
you are
love
everyday you can
be baptized again
everyday can be
your birthday

i can't decide to know
if i am blind or brave
death doesn't scare
or shake me
endings are new beginnings
what kind of clouds
do evaporated dreams create

my body is the holiest temple
and the most gruesome prison

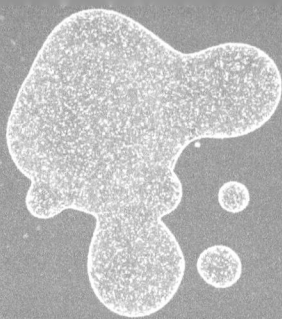

love does not need
an understanding
love just is
love is just
just love
is love
in love

it's not about my naked body
do you realize?
the weight these bones have carried
the life this body has been given
and taken to and from me
i can't help my soul wants to show off
she made it this far for now
have you ever surrendered?
just so you didn't meet your last breath
have you ever surrendered?
just so you can change the weather
only seven minutes to get to heaven

my body is the begging bowl
your love covers me
ashes and ashes
i pretend my hands are yours
painting
in devotion
to the great one
ashes and ashes
take off your jewelry
disrobe
sing between the fire and river
dance between life and death
don't leave my bowl empty
please
i will dwell in your forest fort
sleep on your bed of thorns and feathers
wild berries and the feasts you leave for me
don't let me leave this place still full
of longing and tears
i am becoming hollow
i throw water on the fire
surrender
ashes and ashes
cover me in yours

the one thing i know for sure
is my love won't save you
the one thing i know for sure
is in the mornings i decide to dream again
the one thing i know for sure
is i search for surrender
through pleasure and pain
why does the pain feel holier somehow?
the one thing i know for sure
is my heart is soft and opening
signal searching for mirror eyes

sitting across from you
studying your eyelashes
the way your lips move

you are making a joke
you look up to see me smile
and i look away

crowded places
empty spaces

patiently becoming
while i search for you

slowly the planets
drawing us together
the timing
we require touch

you break me into a million
the same as he did
but different like this
not with your fists
not with your words
not with your power

it's the way you look into my eyes
your fists only hold my heart
your words only whisper love
your power feeds mine

when you barely touch me
sometimes i feel this the most

am i supposed
to play it cool
and not let you know
how i love you so
but i can't wait anymore
i don't want to pretend
that i'm not dying inside
when you found me
touching my arm
touching my lips
and everything
i missed was there
can we be thankful to
just live long enough?
not everyone laughed and cried
or lived long enough to get wrinkles
not every tree loses its leaves in the fall
and gets to change into all the colors

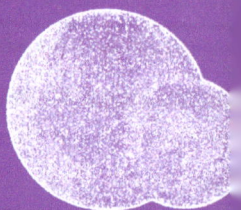

safewords like
it's okay to cry
i will hold you
you are beautiful
i like your darkness too
our love is forever true

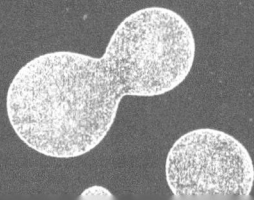

so we just sing each other's name
again and again
love won't spill from our lips any other way
being so hurt this time won't happen
we take our time
whispering secrets
exchanging dreams while we sleep
walking off the trails
jumping into the sea
laughing and crying
not really saying anything
just learning to be

we both know
nothing can change the past
we both know
sand castles don't last

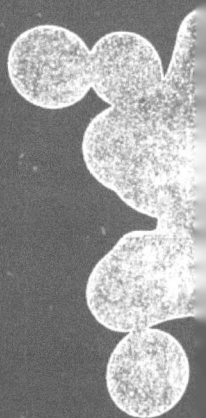

right palm on my neck
fingers finding
new space
only you know the ways
to suffocate and open
the moments
influencing time

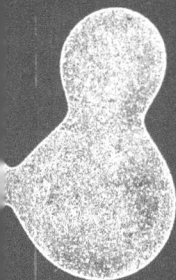

in the mornings
everything is true
no part left untouched
brushing skin
massaging bellies
safer than before
howling sounds
to savor this moment
now
it's all we have
places we are scared to go
softer in this light
finding the demons
and we name them
beautiful things

i want to be rewarded
in titles and names
i want you to call me
submissive and goddess
and peach and pussy cat
call me cunt and slut
worship me
i am your queen
you can give me
a thousand names
i trust you
good girl
bad girl
your girl
i'll call you all mine

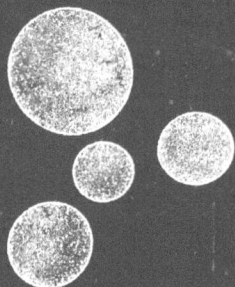

i will change everything
and nothing for you
forever in the palm of your hand

look into my eyes
what do you see
would you stay long enough
to see the real me
would you let yourself
really be seen
would you start to breathe
in and out with me
watch me turn into a lion
and a lamb
feel yourself merge
with infinity

quiet sundays that turn into weeks
centuries of timelessness
reading out loud
while i touch your body
fingertips to skin
hands to heartbeats
legs knotting
making crepes naked
steeping your favorite tea
so i can nourish you
and nap and dream
and wake to your hands
your arms around me
and write in the late afternoon
about the ways you fill me
all the ways you fulfill me
all the ways i let you in
all the ways we break our hearts
open again and again
always opening again

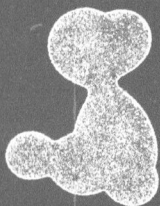

how do you let me feel
brand new and at home
all at once
once there was a time
now there is only illusion

sometimes i mistake someone
else's love for yours but nobody
has your heart

our love is something called poetry

i love you the way
you can always be free
it's okay to like other girls
just please say you'll
never stop loving me

i want you to draw me
paint me
rename me
i am your canvas
i give you permission
to take me
to make me
squeeze me until the last drop
please never stop
i give you permission
i am yours in full submission
we call this game
blanket consent

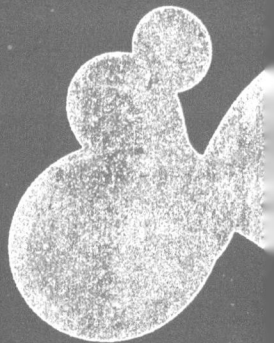

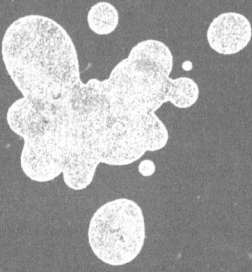

sunsets are nice
but i would be with you
in the dark for lifetimes
or any day
when our eyes meet
colors fall from them anyway

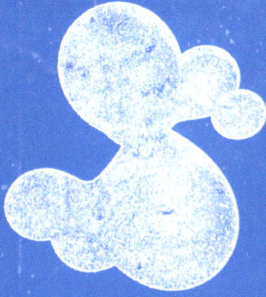

how i open to you
again and again
never how i expect
and that's okay
i am dropping expectations
slowly
it's a process

how does it feel?
my heart beating inside your chest

how does it feel?
my breath in your lungs

how does it feel?
painting the world with our dreams

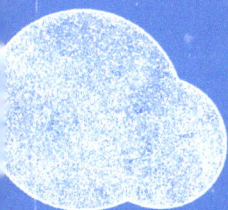

swimming the seas with you
walking the jungles with you
planting gardens with you
holding hearts for lifetimes with you

and i love you
you tell me we are soul mates
and we sit
not touching
but being held just the same
there is nothing more
be still
listen
our hearts beat
our heart beats

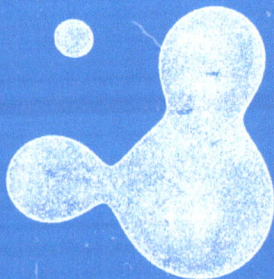

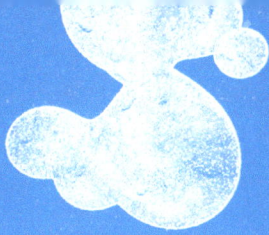

be my silent lover
words take up space
i'm full from you

don't speak or even whisper
we will create waves
in our ocean

silence is our song
fragrances from nectar
pressing wildflowers

between paper
because there are no words
just four letters

you feel like her
you say this to me
do you know what i mean?
you just feel like her
the one i know
i know i know
i know less because i understand more
nothing to solve because
there is nothing to resolve
soften your belly
soften your heart
soften the ways it's okay to fall apart
it's okay to stay up all night
it's okay to fall in love
but don't you want to rise
don't you want to expand into fractals
i feel like her because i am
i am the ritual

i feel like her because i worship
the moment even in the darkness
pitch black
telepathic visions
subtle body messages
and i ask you if i can stay with you
and i ask if i can lay in bed with you
and i ask about the past and you
and then turn off the lights
and fingers dance with you
here there is no final destination
here there is no limits to how we grow
to what i will write about

(continued)

i promise if you look inside
you will figure it out
watch the way i breathe
learn to hold space with me
i want to watch you turn into bliss
i want to watch you make a mess
i want to taste you all over
lick you sober
something about
being here turns me into fire
you feel warm you say
like her
warm thighs like her
soft chest like her
soft edges and new spaces
safe words and invisible places

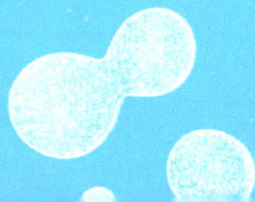

you watch me make
breakfast at midnight
the clocks stop
the oven cools
we sink into the couch
into each other

you tell me to smile and be cute
to be pretty and quiet
but what if i never wanted to
be anything but the truth
which is sometimes
ugly loud uncomfortable
but i found out that's okay too
this is called the whole truth

can't we just play?
kiss until the skies turn grey
feel the raindrops on your skin
the canopy of trees illusion of protection
we find the caves and peel skin off fruit
i'll sew the curtains and sleep on the ground
until you finish the floor
my love is patient but i always want your lips
three walls to hang mirrors and art
the fourth only a door
it's stays open
we are staying open
front porch swinging
sucking on your fingers
listening to the songs of the birds
mostly they sing about being brave
becoming still and soft and
heavy and full of purpose
we drink our nectar
eat figs and berries from the gardens
we keep planting trees, not a wasted seed
peaches and tomatoes
chocolate beans
there is just something about being free

in stillness i feel you
in silence i hear you

i want you here with me
why am i so afraid to say
what i'm feeling?
my whole body is numb
but i'm still full of feelings
my whole body is numb
but i still want you to touch me
find the places and reawaken me
my lips are tingling
and i still want to kiss you endlessly
the ways you take care of me
the ways you love on me
teaching me just how to be so patiently
how to trust endlessly
my whole body is numb
and i want you to come find me
i want you here with me
if i repeat it enough times it will be so
come play with me
come laugh with me
come inside me

(continued)

i will let you come inside me
for a couple of hours be one with me
for a couple of lifetimes
become one with me
am i selfish for the amount
of times i've said me
am i selfish because
i want something so badly
i want you so badly
my whole body is numb
but i can write still
my whole body is numb
but i need you still
my throat is numb
but i can call you still
my throat is numb
but i can swallow still
my chest is numb
but my heart is beating still
my cheeks are numb
but they feel tears falling still
am i numb so i can feel in
between this
and that and this and that
to realize no i can't delay
this moment is the medicine
can we know we are so simple
and whole and holy and holy
this moment is the medicine
and we are so holy

i just want to be cooking
breakfast and dinner for you
living in no pants for you

i like the way you watch me
making beds
and spreading my legs
standing on my head

the way i demand you lay on top
to pin me down
the weight of your body

moving all the used
air out
of my lungs

(continued)

stories being rewritten
you put fingers
in my mouth
telling me not
to make a sound.

you know i like to moan
i need to tell you what i like
how i like to play

i like to play
this way
wrapping our legs together

pretending in a false forever
i like to play in water
i want to dry in the sun

i promise this only way i play
not for keeps
just for fun

the one who leads me
to my breath
the fullness of depth
you bring me into my body
and i would never really
know joy without you
i could never know bliss before you
you teach me the edge
swords hanging above my head
you're kissing me like something
i never knew how to play until you
concrete skinning our knees
and we're laughing
you like how i bleed
i like how it reminds me of
everything moving so quickly
falling from trees
the times we almost drown in the sea
gripping my hands harder
into the sharp rocks
while you are fucking me
buying leather and ropes
begging tighter please
begging for someone
to bring you back to me
more please
the safe words are a mystery
they are just made of sounds
so you have to watch the bodies
we are just made of sounds
so you learn to listen and feel into the bodies

learning love in
a new way
i don't let other people have so
much control over me
i like to be bitten and flipped
and shaken a bit
it reminds me not to hold on so tight
to loosen the grips
drop the oars and raise the sail
forgive easily
surrender so completely
fuck me madly
play out the emotions in motion
rocking the spines
rocking the foundations
relearning what love is
curled tongues and rosey cheeks
blood rising to the surface
the truth on the surface
naked and tangled in
something more than just yourself
i don't want to back track
i don't want to go backwards
let us be here with ourselves now

you said you wanted me
to be yours always
but knew i was all mine
forever
this is nectar
of sovereignty

eat me alive
(i want you too)

memorize me
memorize the feelings
and you know i like to play pretend
to be angry but really
i want you to fuck the madness out of me
to be sad but really
i want you to fuck me softly
my spirituality is my sexuality
does my spirituality measure me?
i will let you open me
i will allow you to soften me
surrendering to trust
you're allowed to blindfold me
handicap me to my knees
surrendering now
learn to just be
a presence
a witness to this scene unfolding
in front of something that is more than me
memorize something now
like the colors behind your closed eyes
the smell of life lingering
the smells of a new box of crayons
old books

(continued)

playing me like a new instrument
something you've never seen before
i'll wiggle like this and make little moans
it's how you learn the tones
you add layers to the bedspread
to stay warm and feel safety
so we buy into the movie club
to go see reels of 55 mils
and sundays we paint each other's skin
and you tie me up for fun
mondays we make plans for the week
and decide to drive nowhere
tuesdays we see how many times
we can cum
wednesdays we write about
the past two days and the future
thursdays we draw little stories
on our bodies
friday is the day of love
they call her venus
we decide to fill her with blanket forts
silent love making
music love making
video taping
and other things until the new day

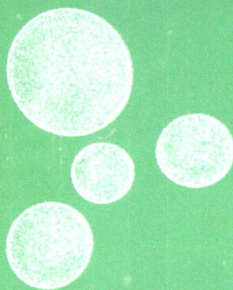

i don't remember my life
before i met you.
i came to you crying for a day
i was remembering a part somehow
looking into eyes that used to be mine

carrying sticks on your back
and smiling like this was
the best moment
because we were alive
a few days later holding hands

and your fingers dancing
and we decided to be quiet and safe
just keep to ourselves
to really remember this time
why do some moments stay?

(continued)

i think of laying next to you
and my body awakens
you can touch me from space
but i still want more memories
i don't want to miss anything
but i do

can you argue with the air?
can you argue with how we feel
something closer to alive again?
something closer than before
i don't remember myself before
i came to you

now i am wondering
how much space you want
do you want me to make your bed
or just get tangled in the sheets?
with your fingers
and presence i'll come for you
and i'll call you a magician
who makes my body sing

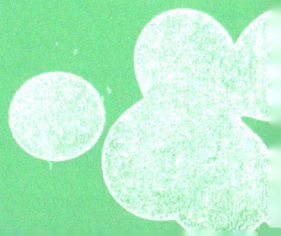

when i say i don't know you
i mean it
i don't want to ever know you
knowing is to be done turning
the pages of the book
every one my favorite
the papers have corners folded
to show how i am still in study
determined
i never want to set you down
turning you in my hands
and examining
the space where your heart beats
the place where my
heart beats now
how could one know
what is always changing
how could i know you?
the being that is breathing
your fragrance whispering
new secrets and fairy tales
my laugh with you
is always brand new
painting my existence
with your fingers
like brush strokes
letting me feel
whole again

(continued)

how is a masterpiece
ever complete
there are too many
details to see
to be
to know you is to wake up
from this dream
so we become still
in the middle of the night
the dance pauses for a moment
we are still
still becoming always
still i love you
each beat of your heart
the next note of the song
the song i don't want to end
so i keep replaying it
learning the words
writing new verses and playing it
on the guitar now
on the trumpet too
you play my ribs like piano keys
and we sing only in tune
dancing to the rhythms
blood pumping
thumping
thinking
how could i have ever
forgotten about you

and so
this morning
sitting on the couch
your legs over mine
you were watching tv
i was holding
onto every second
watching the leg hair
move with your breath
the gentle life
of love sitting before me
full of peace
legs on me
legs on me

the weight of life
let me be here
feeling the weight
let me be here
hearing your breath
let me be here
watching the tv reflecting
off your eyes
watching your face
change with the emotions
of my heart
of the picture show

(continued)

let me be here for
as long as i want
until i fall asleep
and wake again
for a hundred days
i stroke your arm
that is closest
i touch your cheek
and ear
i feel into my fingertips

finding the space
between us
the space between
your weight
and my body
the space between
this moment
and forever
the space
between my life
and yours
the space
between love
and air

II.

THE MANUSCRIPT

selected writing

I keep looking for words
Something new to show you
How or a sign
And a white bird flies in front of me

Do you know what I mean now

I can't decide to know
If I am blind or brave
Death doesn't scare me or terrify me
Endings are new beginning
What kind of clouds
Do evaporate dreams create

I've never done this before
You tell me the rules
Tell me the games to follow

I don't know who to be anymore
He said
You be you and everything is yours

I feel so many things about you
I want you to want me
And not too much
And stay but don't look so close
And touch me mostly always
Except when I don't want you to
I want you to be free
And only want me
To be free
Only craving me though
Only me though

When I miss you, I kiss my own hand.
When I ask why, I hear your answer.
I drown myself in the sunsets,
revive myself before the sunrises,
I use the thing that shocks your heart...
back to this life, back to this life
so I may meet you again.
Will it always be this way?
The colors and clouds
The music that we play.
The blanket we are stitching together.
Will it always be this way?
Holding our hearts, chests and breaths.
Never again you say.

I wake up with your hands all over me
I can't find my skin.

Dear pain
You are temporary
You make me stronger
You allow me to grow
You show me where I am hurting
You bring me closer to myself
You are my secret keeper
You are my fable teller.
Thank you for being my teacher

I feel so far away
Like you have forgotten about me again
I fantasize about scolding you
Sitting in front of my mirror practicing
Then closing my hands
Running my hands on my face
Pretending they are yours
Down my neck
Fingertips on collarbones
Don't forget the way you play my bones
Drawing the lines on my face from worry
Why don't you worry about me?
Leaving me alone again
Talking to myself again
Singing songs in the dark again

And I said no
I said no a lot
It might have been the only word I used
That and please
And I struggled
And I struggled
I struggled a lot
And then i surrendered
I lay there
Being taken away
My soul retreating
Please
I watched myself crumbled and unfolded
crumbled and unfolded again
And crumbled again
Unfolded
Until I am soft paper

So I keep kissing other guys
Because I want you
to claim me to walk
in the door and throw me
Over your shoulder

My lips won't stop but
I keep my eyes shut tight
Because I want them to turn into you
I want you to turn into them.

They want me to be theirs.

You just want me to be.
And I love you so much
I just want you to be free

I know forgiveness like this
The same ways I know of suicide
Both deaths of something you thought was
But had to end to move forward
Both quiet and uncertain
But their bellies full of satisfaction
 Full of the loveliness ache of a full life

I just want to be cooking
breakfast and dinner for you
Living in no pants for you
I like the way you watch me
Making beds spreading my legs
Standing on my head
The way I demand you
lay on top to pin me down
The weight of your body
moving all the used
air out. Of my lungs.
Stories being rewritten.
Or put your fingers in my mouth
Telling me not to make a sound
You know I like to moan
I'll do it quietly in your ear
I need to tell you what I like
How I like to play.
I like to play. This way.
Wrapping our legs together.
Pretending in a false forever.
I like to play in water.
I want to dry in the sun.
I promise the only way I play.
Is not for keeps, just for fun.

Now that you have awaken me
Who will rock me back to sleep

You love me and left
No different then the rest

You think I am a permanent
piece to your art collection
More then a passing sketch
Something that you return to see again
To marvel at.
Think about touching
Second guessing so the oils from your
fingertips won't destroy me too soon
Laying in satin sheets
Salty pillows
Alone and alone with your thoughts
of what you are scared to loose
also you never claimed
This life is yours. Free yourself
from the stories.
You know how you can return here
To the home you build in my lungs
Wallpapering them one strip at a time
One moment at a time
Suffocating me slowly
With the glue
That is bonding me to you

I will change everything
and nothing for you
I will fly for 24 hours
but you have to pick me up
From the airport
Sweep me off my feet
I will worship you until
the sun doesn't shine
Anymore and forever
you will drop petals at my feet
Until I fall asleep
Forever
In your palm
Take me to the sea
Let me walk slowly
 and roll down the hills
Let me follow you
picking berries along the trials
I need you to find shelter
so I can dig in the sand
Looking for treasure
Again
And swim
again
until the sharks start to come in
We watch them and wonder
Why we can't remember
How we used to be them

The way I study your hands
Please let me know every single cell
Let me memory be clear
so I replay the sensation
Of your fingers touching my face
My lips
My smile
My eyelids and ears
My neck, they study me
Like I want to remember the way your eyes
your eyes looking at me
Looking into mine
You promise me a kiss
Making sure I get to taste you
forever
Pausing
For a moment
Pausing
So I can close my eyes and meet you here
In this place where I know all of you
In this place where you hold all of me.

You want to dress like
a skeleton for Halloween
So we can see each other's bones now
So we will recognize each other then
When this moment is past
And a breath became a last

So I pretend to text you
and call you in the middle of the night
I wake up from good and bad dreams
and you are never by my side.
So I am here to have fun.
Beat this heart until it's done.
And I promise to make promises
To make promises forever
Looking into your eyes
Holding your hand
Holding your skin
Together again

What if the parts of you
that you want to hide
are the parts the world needs the most?

Let me witness you
Love me and let me be
Free

You know what toxic is
You just don't know yet
You are good enough
Smart brave funny pretty strong enough
You are enough
To walk away
To learn the lesson
To fill in the blank

How do we create newness?
How do I make room for more love?

Clear the stale.
Exhale and clear the air.
From my lungs.
Exhale and clear your stories
From the space between my ears

I take the layers of you off me
I start in the shower
Then my bedroom
Crying into my pillow until I'm dry
Looking into my mirror until I cry
Again
So I touch myself like I want the next one to
So I love myself like I want someone to

I go to dinner
At my favorite place
I think about how I will cook the next one dinner
And how he will kiss on my face
How we will fall in love so quickly
And never think of being replaced

Again and again
We decide to flirt with others
And pretend we are new lovers
We dress up to play
We write love letters
Promising to not over stay
We go downtown
Make love in an alley
We still can't leave each other's side
So we decide to just be alive

I thought I had to climb the mountain
To be free and pretty

Trying to climb out
of the muddy steep valley.
Sinking and staining myself
When I surrendered.
Lay down, allowed myself to become
The flowers on the hillside
I found I was nourished
in the spring of the valley

How do I wash you from my skin?
I scrub until my sponge starts to bleed.
Filling the tub
With blood
With the plans.
With my fear of loneliness.
I would rather be alone then suffocating.
I would rather be alone then die having never lived.

If you want to leave.
Leave.
Make the decision and the world shifts.
Take all the time you need.
You know when your moment is here.
Walk away and say thank you.
To yourself.
To your heart that is still beating.
To your life that is unfolding.

Why?
 Is a stone different from a rock.
Is my love never enough for you.

Both hard and etched by water.
Cold and hot.
Crumbles in your hand or the densest matter.

Crystalline molecules.
Made to withstand the movement of time.

One time I flew to London to find Waldo
I found him
Faceless
Heart beating faintly
Not nearly enough
to penetrate this rainbow body
Not nearly enough to fill my dreams
He was 2 D cheap paper and rose art markers
I am pressed wildflowers painted with watercolors
Highly pigmented
Rare
7D
Love endlessly

I am

Selfish
Self (ones being)
Ish (to be close to)

You are pretty enough to say no
You are strong enough to walk away
You are brave enough to start again
You are human enough to cry
You are smart enough to know the truth
Which is you are enough
You are enough

Take your shoes off
Lay on your back
Raise your feet toward the sky or ceiling
Squeeze and open your toes
Roll your ankles
Start silently thanking your toes and feet
Thank your legs
Start thanking whatever is above you
Say thank you to whatever is below you
To the place you are in say thank you
Expand beyond the place you are
Send your thank yous endlessly outward
Notice the breath moving your body
Feel it move through your nostrils
In and out
Again and again
Notice your heart beating
Start singing thank yous
To every cell of your living being
Notice how your body starts to sing back

When life is scary
I go to the water
To remember
the art of how to be
Water on skin
Washing the dishes
Taking a bath
Or swimming in the sea
It's all the same to me
She always reveals
There is no real mystery

You think I am yours
So I owe you my body
My nights all with you
Suffocating
Sinking into the over priced couch
In the over priced house
I planted a tree in the backyard
I have picked the fruit twice and
I could walk away now
Your cold touches are killing my blooms
Your screams are my jaw aches
Headaches heartaches
I will love you the way my mom taught me how
You how yours taught you
Ands it's dark. And it's cold
Even though we paid the electricity bill
And the house is flooded
The plumber cashed the check
He repaired the pipes
And we are still drowning
in someone else dream

Ill make all these promises
these promises
I will get old and grey for you
Wrinkled and brittle one day for you
I'll love to be one hundred and eight for you
For you
I promise to dance and sing
Put my feet in wet grass
Swim in our special place
Make the world our special place
I'll breathe for you
I'll inhale
And let myself write you letters
Send you notes like you were reading them
Because you read them
Please let me know you read them
Because I promise
One I'll stop crying for you
And start only smiling for you
I'll eat fruits in season for you
For you
I'll close my eyes and taste them
Juice on my lips
You on my lips
Maybe I'll eat the skins too
Like I was brand new
I promise
I'll feel this world
Like I was brand new
Every note of this song
I promise
For you
For you

Let me tell you all what I do
Read and write and sleep sometimes
Always always thinking of you

I wrapped my arms around loneliness
Until I realized I was hugging myself

I don't want to be scared
but I am running wild and naked in the jungle
You want to control your words and fists
But you are not able to face demons like this
I don't want to be small anymore
but my ribs keep collapsing onto my heart
You want to forgive your dad
But you don't know how to stop hate
I don't want us to end
But I am meant to live beyond this story
You want a happily ever after
But you forgot to keep breathing
You stopped breathing

I was scared to see you again
Scared your fist would meet my face
My name would fall from your lips
Your heart would melt back into mine

Then I found out you were gone already
You left just before I arrived
You kept the same phone number
You stopped answering
You stopped checking the voicemails
I stopped blocking my number
You still won't answer
And now I know
We have nothing to be scared of

Sitting across from you
Studying your eyelashes
The way your lips move

You are making a joke
You look up to see me smile
And I look away

Put some makeup on
Or don't wear any
Wear pretty underwear
Or none
Take yourself to eat at a place
To savor the quiet
and enjoy your legs touching each other
Have a drink
Of chai or Prosecco or water
Go dance
Just dance go home alone
Or with someone
Only if you like them
No matter what look in the mirror
And say I love you a few times in the morning

I can't
Stop my lips from kissing
I just close my eyes and pretend it's you

I quietly hang my art in galleries
Plant seeds and seeds
I write poems endlessly
Not to be seen
No I don't want you to see me
I want you to close your eyes
And put your hand on your ribs
Feel your body being breathed
Start saying thank you.
Open your eyes
Be loud in the gallery
Shake the tree until the fruit falls
Sing the lyrics so loudly
So loudly
Won't you please
Until you can only taste me

I am not here waiting for you anymore
I know you
I am searching for the littlest smallest hidden
Pockets of love
That live in this life
That make home in what we call loneliness
That make love it what we call despair
and hope
I have met you in my dreams
I fall asleep and feel you with me
I drive my car and you watch me dance and sing
I want to stop this maddening pace
And you take me to the mirror
To see you in my face

I want to be rewarded in titles
I want you to call me good and goddess
And peach and pussy cat
Call me a cunt ad a slut
Worship me, I am your queen.
You can give me a thousand names
I trust you
Good girl
Bad girl
Your girl

I make my life a meditation
Always going back
To the sensations of the skin
Water and air
Noticing ribs
lungs
Saying thank you
Learning to live as a prayer

Learning to watch the bodies
Of bones and something we can see
Of emotions. Identify with what we are feeling.
What happens when we take the suffering away?
What happens when these bodies
collapse one day? How long until they are gone?
Who will be left with what is real.
Maybe it's just a reel.
The soundtrack,
The great one's endless soul's song

Who is listening now?
Who is watching this picture now?
Who is dancing in the light and shadows now?
Be quiet, and dance, and listen to the song
Playing right now.

I want you to draw me
Paint on me
Rename me
I am your canvas
I give you permission
To take me
To make me
Squeeze me until the last drop
Please please never stop
I give you permission
I am yours in submission

I just want you
to hold my hand at lunch
Listen to me hummm
Grind against me at shows
Play with my hair while I masturbate
Watch me dance
Watch me play

Look into my eyes
Look into my eyes
Look into my eyes

My teacher
Of love
This breath
The air
To be love is to become
Formless
Nameless
Invisible
Force
Subtle
Timeless
Everything is suspended
In love
In this breath
In this invisible air
Holding us together

I will never settle for the shore
I am the queen of the sea

I close my eyes and go back to you
anytime
We are timeless
Boulders to pebbles
Pebbles to smaller pebbles.
Tumbling still, dreaming of becoming sand.
The sounds under the water.
Better then the symphony
We sat towards the back, dressed up
Here I am naked and there is no intermission
No one to give me permission
To move
To swim
To dance
To sing how I will forever love you

I want a love that makes mix tapes,
writes me pretty love notes,
I don't need plans and promises for the future.
All I need is stars and waves next to the sea.
Just your heartbeat next to mine endlessly.

I go watch sunsets with your sister still
Nobody cares where the other is
What's happening
Our bones are together
And we sit still, so so quietly.
You would never even hear us
And we think about the all the ways we forgive
To forgive ourselves and you and him and life
Like if we are silent long enough
the nightmares will die
or we will forgive our selves for being a part of it
How did we come up with the equation
that ended with us black and blue
and lips stitched shut with ribs stitched shut.
Stitched shut. Stitched shut.
Invisible shackles
Imagining the worst so we can laugh
about the funny things we could find there
Even with our mouths bound in shame
we found ways to laugh and hum and call to the water
It keeps us warm from the inside out
Even on the sunniest day we look for the owls
Feathers on the ground and holes in the trees.
How we are full of life and then dead.
Dirt under our fingernails and then divine.
Invisible sunsets and planets rotating a star
Don't define us anymore

Finding the space between us.
The space between your weight and my body
The space between this moment and forever
The space between my life and yours
The space between love and air

Riding on the train with you
Your legs squeeze mine
Like a vine that wants to grow
You look for where you can land
Is it safe here?

You fall asleep on my shoulder.
You feel safe here.
I practice feeling safe here.

Sometimes I wake up and smell like you
That's how I know you live in my dreams too

I keep falling in love and getting
my heart broken on the same day.
All I want to do is play.

How can you tell me I am perfect
Then throw your fist at me
From the same chair.
Is it because I endure the same pain you did.
I sit and cry and then rise and forgive you.
Our difference is I stayed to defeat the dragon.
And she told me how we all came from love.

You tell me to smile and be cute
To be pretty and quiet
But what if I never wanted to
Be anything but the truth
Which is sometimes
Ugly loud uncomfortable
But I found a way that can be sparkly too

My love for you doesn't stop
because you left my side.
My love doesn't know
your lips prefer another's.
My love doesn't listen
when told to be contained.
My love won't stop singing
about the depth of her ocean.
My love, my love, doesn't ask questions.
My love, my love, is only supreme.

One time I tasted my tears and dove into the sea
I remembered all the gifts you have ever given to me

At times I wish that life wasn't a dream
Everything projected on a movie screen

Created sustainer producer and movie director
The actors reflections reflections
of inner sensations

And I can't stop writing you letters
And I can't stop singing our songs
And I don't care about formalities and rsvps
And I don't care if i cry about everything
And there is a dream after this one
And there is a life after this one
And maybe it's more real then your nightmares
And maybe it's more then you could imagine
And perhaps I decided to play in the wet grass
And perhaps I decided to do laundry at the shore
And sometimes I wonder if my cat feels my heart
And sometimes I wonder if you read my mind
And then I realize the falling stars are not stars
And then I realize the river is my home
And my grandfathers garden is overgrown now
And my grandmother's heart is with me now
And my children carry them in their bones now
And my life is because of theirs now
And my blood is thick like god's now

Those dreams when you climb into my bed
Your voice gets stuck in my head
And I feel you so close
And I want you to come
I want you to guide me
I surrender to the great ones will
I'm hallow like bamboo
Something so beautiful you long to fulfill
Destiny or will something people say
Time isn't real
so there's just nowhere to go
I promise you I can't promise anything.

III.

PHOTOGRAPHY

www.ingramcontent.com/pod-product-compliance
Lightning Source LLC
Chambersburg PA
CBHW041958090426
42811CB00025B/1927/J